Stuff
to know
when you start
school

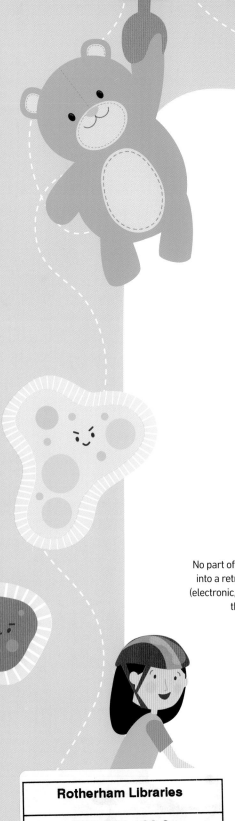

Penguin
Random
House

Editor Hélène Hilton
Design and Illustration Charlotte Bull
Editorial Assistance Violet Peto
Additional Design and Illustration Rachael Hare
Producer, Pre-Production Dragana Puvacic
Producer John Casey
Educational Consultant Penny Coltman
Jacket Designer Charlotte Bull
Jacket Coordinator Francesca Young
Managing Editor Penny Smith
Managing Art Editor Mabel Chan
Publisher Mary Ling
Art Director Jane Bull

First published in Great Britain in 2018 by
Dorling Kindersley Limited
80 Strand, London, WC2R 0RL

A CIP catalogue record for this book
is available from the British Library.
ISBN: 978-0-2413-1618-4

Printed and bound in China

A WORLD OF IDEAS:
SEE ALL THERE IS TO KNOW

www.dk.com

Contents

All about you!

From the colour of your eyes to the shape of your nose, you are one of a kind from the day you are born. And every day since then, you've become even more special.

No one in the whole world looks like you. We all have different faces and bodies, as well as different hair, eye, and skin colours.

You are completely unique, totally special, and perfectly you.

No matter how you look, you are perfect just as you are.

All the things that you like, from your favourite toys to the friends and family you love, also make you who you are.

The choices you make are also a part of you. Being kind and friendly are choices that you make every day. What will you choose today?

Here are some ways you can practise.

Your name is who you are!

Practise writing the letters in your name to learn how to spell it.

With a pen or pencil on paper

In the air with your finger

In a steamed-up mirror or window

With a stick in the sand

With pebbles

With playdough

Who's in your family?

Your family is made up of the people who look after you, make you feel safe, and love you no matter what.

Hello! I live with my mum and dad.

Hey! I have a mum, a dad, two sisters, and three brothers.

Hi! I was adopted by my mum and dad.

Hi! My sisters and I have two dads who look after us.

Each family is different and special.

Hello! My mum takes care of my brother and me.

Hey! I live with my mum, my stepdad, and stepbrother.

New siblings

Is there a new baby in your family?

Congratulations!

Here are some things you can do together to be friends.

Cuddle the baby.

Play with the baby.

Read to the baby.

Talk to the baby.

Babies cry because they can't talk yet, but babies can understand words before they can speak. Chat to your baby to help them learn faster.

How do you feel today?

Emotions are important because they tell you how you feel. All your feelings are worth listening to.

happy

tired

scared

calm

Face game

Can you guess how the people around you are feeling today?
How can you tell?

excited

I'm all shy!

If you feel shy, sometimes words just don't want to come out. That's okay, you just need to take a deep breath. You will get more confident with some practise.

nervous

angry

If I get very upset my emotions want to come out all at once! I take a breath to calm down and use my words to say how I feel.

Look at all these emotions. Can you think of things that make you feel like this?

lonely

sad

grumpy

embarrassed

What are tears?

Tears are drops of salty water that come from a pouch near the eye. People cry when they are sad or hurt, but also if they are happy and laughing. Weird!

9

Hello!

It's nice to meet you.

Saying "hello" is a nice way to greet someone.

Very important manners

Being **polite** shows others that you **care** about their feelings. Your best manners make people **smile**!

Ask nicely by saying "**please**".

Please

can you help me?

Thank you

for my present! I love it!

Saying "**thank you**" shows that you are grateful.

If you need to interrupt someone or get their attention, say **"excuse me"**.

Bye!
See you later!

Don't forget to say **"goodbye"** when you leave.

Excuse me!
This is really important.

I am really, really **sorry** I hurt your feelings.

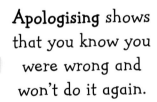

Apologising shows that you know you were wrong and won't do it again.

Nervous giggles

Lots of children giggle when they are told off because they feel embarrassed. If this happens to you, try to stay calm and listen so that you can learn.

Put your **legs** in the two small holes of your **underpants**.

Socks go on your feet

Pants go first

Useful things to know when you get dressed.

Left

Right

Do gloves go on your ears?

No! Gloves go on your hands!

Shoes go on this way round.

Put your **feet here!**

Shoelaces can be tricky when you start off,
so ask someone to show you how to do it.
If you practise lots you'll be doing
your own laces very soon!

Zip or buttons?

Most buttons are done
up by putting the button
through the **buttonhole.**

Zips are made up of little
teeth that come together
to close. Pull the zip up to
bring the teeth together.

Check the label so you put
your top the right way round.
The label goes in the back.

Try laying out your clothes on the
floor before putting them on to
make sure they're not inside out.

What will you wear today?

Pick the perfect clothes for you to wear today.

Spring

In **spring**, there are showers and rainbows. **Can you find a raincoat, welly boots, an umbrella, and a rain hat?**

Summer

In **summer**, the weather is sunny and hot. **Can you find a sunhat, sunglasses, shorts, a T-shirt, and sandals?**

Autumn

In **autumn**, the weather is cool and windy.
Can you find a jumper, a scarf, trousers, and shoes?

Winter

In **winter**, it's cold and it sometimes snows.
Can you find snow boots, a coat, a woolly hat, and gloves?

15

Squeaky clean
from head to toe

Here's a little guide to making sure you always feel (and smell) as fresh as a daisy.

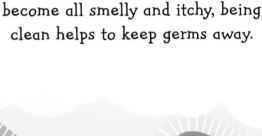

Germs are tiny little things that can make you feel **poorly**.

But WHY do I have to be clean?

Apart from making sure you don't become all smelly and itchy, being clean helps to keep germs away.

Tissues ready!

Blow your nose by closing your mouth and blowing as hard as you can, out of your nostrils into a tissue.

Don't forget to throw tissues in the bin!

Catch those germs!

Cover your mouth when you cough to stop germs spreading to other people. Then wash your hands.

Wash your hands!

Keep your hands germ-free with lots of soap and water, especially before eating.

Look after your nails

Your nails keep growing all the time. Have them clipped to keep them short and tidy.

Shower time

Take a shower or a bath to wash yourself with lots of soap. Make shower time more fun by singing as loudly as you can!

Brush your hair

Brush or comb your hair to keep it from getting all tangled.

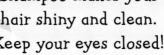

Shampoo makes your hair shiny and clean. Keep your eyes closed!

Hello, teeth!

I'm a front tooth, an **incisor**. My sharp edge cuts food.

I'm a side tooth, a **canine**. I am pointy to tear food.

I'm a big back tooth, a **molar**. I mash food into tiny bits.

Sparkly teeth

Your teeth need you to look after them so they stay **healthy** and sparkling. Brush them **twice a day** for **two whole minutes**.

Dentists are special teeth doctors. They check and clean your teeth to make sure they are healthy.

Wobbly tooth

When you're ready for grown-up teeth, your milk teeth get all wobbly and fall out. That makes a space for your big teeth!

But WHY should I brush my teeth?

Brushing helps to protect your teeth against germs that make little holes (cavities) in your teeth.

Sugary things like fizzy drinks and sweets can also damage your teeth.

How to brush your teeth (and do a really, really good job)

1 Squeeze a little blob of toothpaste onto your toothbrush.

2 Move your brush up and down over your teeth.

3 Keep brushing for two minutes, making sure you brush the front, back, and underneath of your teeth.

4 Spit out the toothpaste and rinse your toothbrush.

5 All done! Your teeth are sparkly clean and minty fresh.

Don't forget to clean between your teeth!

19

Toilet time

If it's time to be out of nappies, it's time to learn what to do with a grown-up toilet.

If you need the toilet, don't wait until it's an emergency.

Toilets outside of houses, like at school or in restaurants, can be different to the toilets you have at home. If you feel unsure about them, check with a grown-up.

1 Sit on the toilet.

2 Do your business.

3 Wipe with toilet paper until you're all clean.

4 Flush!

5 Wash your hands.

Carefully, with soap and water. (EVERY TIME!)

If you do have an accident, ask a grown-up to help you get clean and dry.

Everyone has little accidents from time to time, especially when you are first out of nappies. Try not to worry!

Try to always go to the toilet right before bedtime.

Night-time accidents

If you have an accident while you sleep, it's not your fault. Lots of children wet the bed so don't be embarrassed. Bed wetting goes away all on its own after a while.

Your first sleepover

Sleepovers are so much fun! Whose house are you sleeping at tonight?

Don't forget your favourite cuddly toy.

Follow the wiggly line to get all ready for bed.

All tucked in

Say good night

Lights out!

Spooky dark

Not being able to see what's around you can be worrying. But if you can't have a night-light, remind yourself that you are safe in your bed.

Put your pyjamas on

Brush your teeth

Bedtime story

Go to the toilet

Sweet dreams

I love sleepovers at my grandparents' house. I always get a bedtime story.

Your amazing body

From the top of your head, to the tips of your toes, your body is perfect.

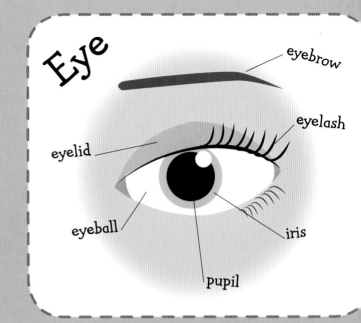

Eye

- eyebrow
- eyelash
- eyelid
- eyeball
- iris
- pupil

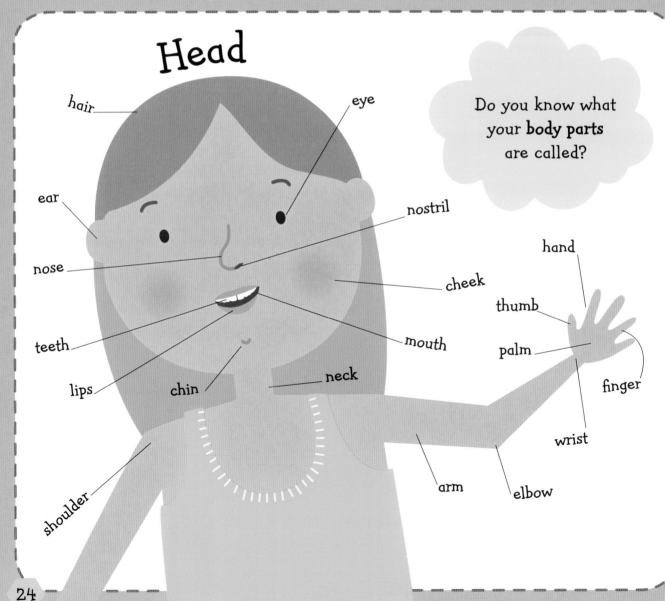

Head

Do you know what your **body parts** are called?

- hair
- eye
- ear
- nostril
- nose
- cheek
- teeth
- mouth
- lips
- chin
- neck
- shoulder
- hand
- thumb
- palm
- finger
- wrist
- arm
- elbow

Body

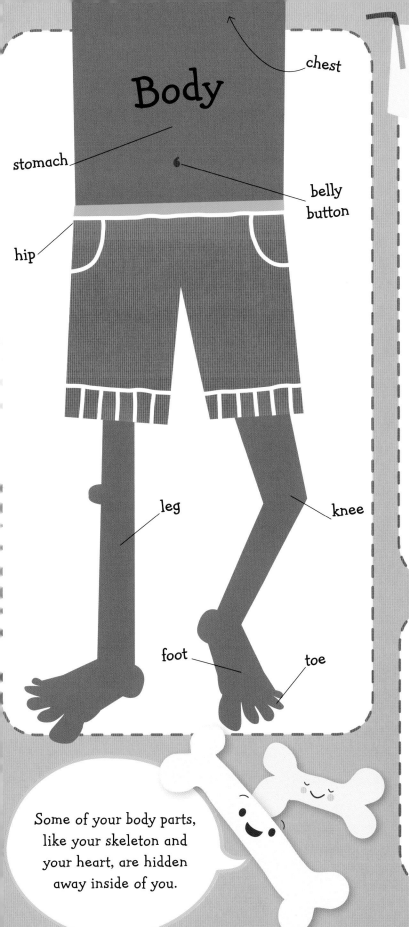

chest

stomach

belly button

hip

leg

knee

foot

toe

Some of your body parts, like your skeleton and your heart, are hidden away inside of you.

Eat well

Your body needs you to eat different types of food to stay strong and healthy. Here are some things you should eat every day:

Lots of **fruit** and **vegetables.**

Some starchy food, like **bread** or **rice.**

Some protein, such as **meat, eggs,** or **beans.**

Some healthy oil, like **avocados** or **nuts.**

Move your body

You are meant to move, run, jump, dance, and use lots of energy. Your body needs to exercise to stay strong.

Happy heart

Feeling happy is one of the
best things in the world!

What makes you happy?

being read to

cuddly toys

hugs

painting

Sleepy time

Your body and your mind
need sleep to feel ready for
a new day. Children need
to sleep for around 10 or 11
hours every night.

family

pets

making friends

Draw a picture of all the things that make you happy. Think about the people who make you smile and the things you love doing.

playing

No one can be happy all the time. The best you can do is to keep trying to be happy as often as you can!

sports

Look at all this food!

There is so much food to try and taste. Which of these are your favourites?

tomatoes

noodles

courgette

broccoli

beetroot

cauliflower

carrot

chilli

peas

corn

potato

sweet potato

bread

rice

orange

strawberries

grapes

pineapple

olive oil

apple

watermelon

blackberries

kiwi

honey

fish

meat

milk

eggs

All the food that we eat either comes from a plant or an animal.

You and the Universe

Our planet Earth is just one tiny weeny little planet in the whole big wide Universe!

Sun

Mercury

Venus

The Moon is not a planet.

Earth

That's where we live!

Mars

Our sun is actually a star, a big ball of burning gas.

Look at the sky at night to see far away stars and planets. No one knows how big the Universe is. It might go on forever and ever.

The Universe is EVERYTHING. It's all of time and space and everything in it.

Sometimes you can spot Mars and other planets in the sky at night. They look tiny because they're so far away.

Saturn

Neptune

Uranus

Jupiter

Earth is the only planet we know of in the whole Universe that has living things (like you) on it.

Our Solar System

Earth is one of eight planets that spin around the Sun. Together they make up the Solar System.

Look after our planet

Our planet Earth looks after us by giving us food, water, and energy. But we also need to look after the Earth before it becomes too damaged.

You can help save our planet Earth.

Paper, cardboard, glass, some metals, and some plastics can be recycled.

That means they can be reused instead of just being rubbish! Isn't that great?

Grow some of your own food or buy food that was grown close to home.

Turn switches off to save energy.

Make your garden friendly to little animals that might need to live there.

What can I do to help?

Plant a tree. Trees make the air cleaner.

Recycle your rubbish.

Walk or cycle rather than drive to save fuel.

Very important living things

There are so many different animals and plants in the world that we still haven't discovered all of them. Which of these do you already know?

hippopotamus

snake

bee

dog

pigeon

butterfly

worm

polar bear

chicken

cat

sunflower

seed

shark

duck

flower

snail

crab

rabbit

Plants and animals are things that are alive.

leaves

ants

tiger

elephant

tree

dragonfly

horse

goldfish

human

frog

Living things need to be looked after. Animals can't talk, but they can feel pain so it's important to be nice to them.

35

Stay safe

You are a very special person so learn to keep yourself safe and sound.

To **cross the road**, hold a grown-up's hand, use a pedestrian crossing, and check both ways for cars.

Watch out for cars!

Be careful around water.

Don't touch electricity.

Wear a **seat belt** when you're in the car.

Hello!

Never speak to **someone you don't know on the Internet or in real life** without checking with a grown-up first.

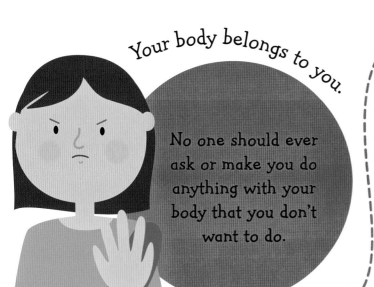

Your body belongs to you.

No one should ever ask or make you do anything with your body that you don't want to do.

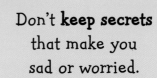

Don't **keep secrets** that make you sad or worried.

If you see anything on a **computer, phone, or tablet** that upsets you, walk away and go and tell you a grown-up.

Don't play near railway lines.

What number should you call in an emergency?

1 2 3
4 5 6
7 8 9
0

Always talk to someone you trust if you are feeling sad or worried.

Here are some people you can talk to:

someone in your family you trust
a police officer
a doctor
a nurse
someone at nursery or school

Sing and sign

Here are some fun songs you can sing
and act out with your hands.

___

Itsy bitsy spider climbed up the waterspout.

Down came the rain and washed the spider out.

Out came the sun and dried up all the rain

And itsy bitsy spider climbed up the spout again.

___

Round and round the garden

Like a teddy bear.

One step, two step,

Tickle you under there.

This little piggy went to market.

This little piggy stayed at home.

This little piggy had roast beef.

This little piggy had none.

And this little piggy went...

"Wee, wee, wee," all the way home.

If you're happy and you know it, clap your hands.

If you're happy and you know it, clap your hands.

If you're happy and you know it,

and you really want to show it.

If you're happy and you know it,

clap your hands!

Sing and learn

Learn some super-useful things
as you sing your little heart out!

You can sing
the Alphabet Song
to the tune of Twinkle,
Twinkle, Little Star.

Alphabet Song

A B C D E F G

H I J K L M N O P

Q R S T U and V

W X Y and Z

Now I know my ABC,

Next time won't you
sing with me?

The Alphabet Song teaches
you the names of all the
letters. Do you know what
sound the letters make
when they are in words?

Fish and count to 10

1, 2, 3, 4, 5,

Once I caught a fish alive.

6, 7, 8, 9, 10

Then I let it go again.

Why did you let it go?

Because it bit my finger so.

Which finger did it bite?

This little finger on my right!

How to be a really good friend

Friends are so much fun!
Here are some tips to make
lots of new friends.

If someone looks sad
or lonely, ask them if
they want to play.

Share your toys
or treats with others.
Then maybe they will
share with you too.

Playing nicely
means being kind
to each other.

NO!

If you've upset someone, try to understand what you have done wrong, and say "sorry".

If someone is being mean to you or to someone else, say "NO!", tell them how they are making you feel, and let a grown-up know straight away.

Take turns so that you can each have a go. Be fair!

What's a bully?

Bullies pick on others. Often bullies are people who don't know how to make friends so they act mean to feel included. If someone is bullying, you should tell a grown-up, but you could also show the bully how to be kind and play nicely.

Look at what I can do!

Here is a whole bunch of **awesome** stuff you can try, too. **You can do it!**

- ☐ Ride a bike or scooter

- ☐ Swim with swimming aids

- ☐ Make an obstacle course

- ☐ Climb a tree (carefully)

- ☐ Build a nature den

- ☐ Make mud art

- ☐ Play catch

- ☐ Go on a colour hunt

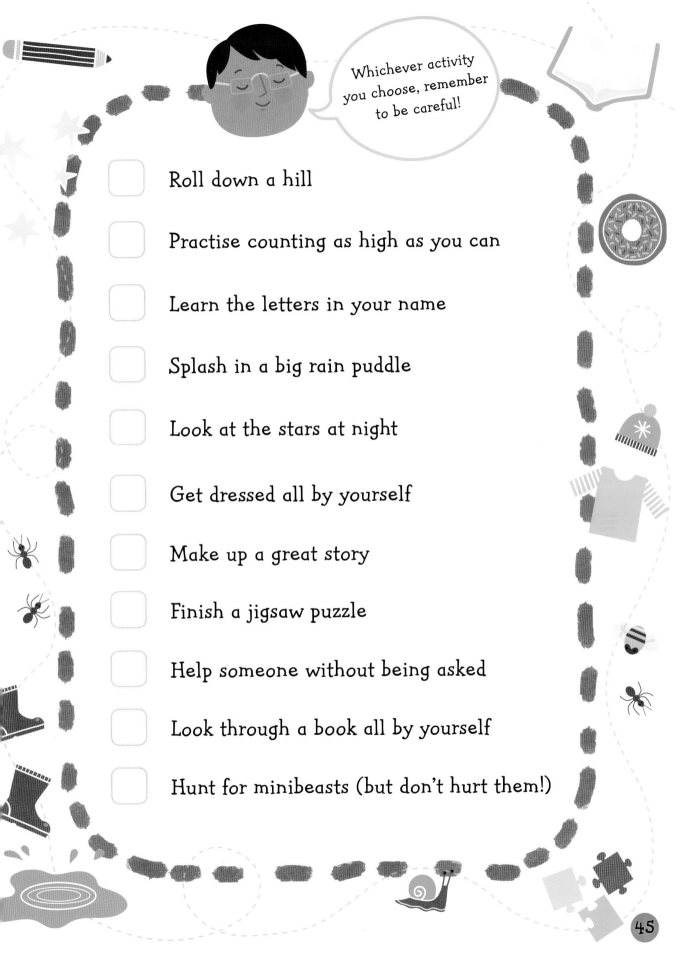

Whichever activity you choose, remember to be careful!

☐ Roll down a hill

☐ Practise counting as high as you can

☐ Learn the letters in your name

☐ Splash in a big rain puddle

☐ Look at the stars at night

☐ Get dressed all by yourself

☐ Make up a great story

☐ Finish a jigsaw puzzle

☐ Help someone without being asked

☐ Look through a book all by yourself

☐ Hunt for minibeasts (but don't hurt them!)

Hello, school!

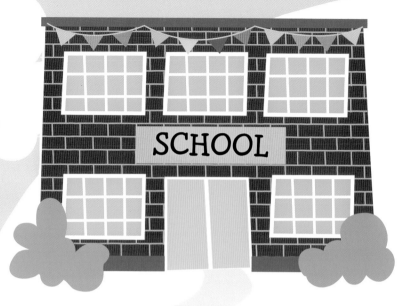

It's your first day of school! There are so many new things to say "hello" to.

Hello, playground

Hello, classroom

Hello,
friends

Hello,
coat peg

Hello,
head teacher

Hello,
teacher

Say "see you later" to Mum and Dad. They'll be back after school.

Hello,
toys

Index

Acknowledgements

The publisher would like to thank the following for
their kind permission to reproduce their photographs:

(Key: a-above; b-below/bottom; c-centre; f-far; l-left; r-right; t-top)

28 Dreamstime.com: Leszek Ogrodnik / Lehu (c, cr); Tracy Decourcy / Rimglow (c/Carrot); Pichest
Boonpanchua / Khumthong (br). **29 Dreamstime.com:** Leszek Ogrodnik / Lehu (ca). Getty Images:
Burazin / Photographer's Choice RF (cra). **34 123RF.com:** Eric Isselee / isselee (crb/Polar bear cub);
Ievgen Kovalev / genjok (cb). **Dreamstime.com:** Irochka (cb/Sunflower); Isselee (crb). **Fotolia:** Eric
Isselee (cl). **35 Dreamstime.com:** Liligraphie (cl); Natalya Aksenova (tc). **iStockphoto.com:** Taalvi (crb)

All other images © Dorling Kindersley
For further information see: www.dkimages.com